Short

Stories

for

Christmas

Arthur F. Fogartie

The Sixteenth Manger

Illustrations by Gary R. Phillips

Judson Press ® Valley Forge

To Mom:

"Her children rise up and call her blessed."

—Proverbs 31:28

THE SIXTEENTH MANGER

Copyright © 1987
Judson Press, Valley Forge, PA 19482–0851

Library of Congress Cataloging-in-Publication Data

Fogartie, Arthur F.
  The sixteenth manger.

  1. Christian stories, American.   I. Title.
PS3556.026S5   1987   813'.54   87-3002
ISBN 1-8170-1119-6

The name JUDSON PRESS is registered as a trademark in the U.S. Patent Office.
Printed in the U.S.A.

Contents

The Sixteenth Manger

*S*TEMSBURG: 180 Miles" I stared at the sign in disbelief. I'd been on the road since 5 P.M. and had only traveled seventy-five miles?

The first half hour had gone smoothly. A flake or two of snow fell, but nothing alarming, and I cruised along at a little over 55 miles per hour. I saw surprisingly little traffic for Christmas Eve—everyone else must have gotten an early start.

The snow came slowly at first, floating listlessly past the headlights and breaking the monotony of the road, but hardly impairing my vision. It seemed kind of nice, actually; it made the night less lonely as it surrounded my car in its moist, chilly blanket.

I must have slowed down unconsciously as the snowfall increased. Now my back ached from hunching over the steering wheel, and my eyes throbbed from constant peering. Let's see—9:30. Good grief! Over the past four hours I'd averaged a blistering 12.5 miles per hour!

"Stemsburg: 180 Miles" *At this rate, I'll make it by New Year's,* I thought. But if the snow kept up. . . .

What started as a pleasant winter drifting had grown into a snarling, wind-whipped blizzard, charging into headlights and windshields as if determined to break through. Just beyond the semicircles cut by the struggling wipers, the snow had already caked several inches thick. Five miles or 180, it didn't matter. I wasn't going to make it home tonight.

* * * * *

The popping of a fresh cedar log on the fire and appetizing aromas tickling my nose woke me up.

"Dozed off for a while, eh, Mister?" Jake Trimble's voice had a hard-working quality to it. "Not that I'm surprised what with the drive you had and all. Say, it's really coming down now—lucky you could even see the house lights. We're the last folks for a couple of miles, but I told you that already I reckon. At least you got a chance to call your family and tell 'em you're okay. Now they won't worry. I know it's 10 o'clock and all, but we always put off eating 'til late on Christmas Eve. You go ahead and rest if you wanna, but if you're up to it, dinner's on."

Four of us surrounded the table: Jake, Anna, Jo-Jo Trimble, and me. Jo-Jo (about eighteen or twenty, I guessed) perched himself on a high, three-legged stool because I got his chair. He had to lean over in a most uncomfortable looking position to eat. I'd have taken the stool, but Jake and Anna insisted.

"We hold hands here, Mister," Jake announced. He clamped his hand on top of mine and started, "Lord, thank you for sending us this traveler so we can do your bidding. Bless us as we eat what you have given. And thank you for your Son, Jesus, our Lord. Amen."

Then, we "had at it" as Jake said. "It" wasn't a lavish meal—certainly not the opulent spread I usually had at Christmas—but the food was well prepared, and Anna made sure I got plenty.

I was surprised by how little Jake and Jo-Jo ate. Both were considerably larger than I, yet their portions seemed smaller than mine. When I took two rolls, they took one, and the second time around, Jake didn't take any.

The conversation suffered mightily from interruptions, most of which focused on me.

"Jake, our guest needs more potatoes."

"Mister, how 'bout some gravy to go with that?"

"Would you pass the butter please—be sure to help yourself first."

"You could probably wash that down a little better if I heated up your coffee, couldn't you, Mister?"

One meal and two slices of mince pie later, I slumped into a fireside rocker, hung over with that all-too-familiar post-holiday-meal drowsiness. After she'd cleared the dishes, Anna made her way across the room from the stove and planted herself squarely in front of the roaring fire.

"Jake," she began, "Thank you for your gift. It was wonderful."

"Excuse me," I butted in, "Did I miss something?"

Anna grinned. "Oh, of course, you wouldn't know. The goose—the goose we had for dinner. That was Jake's gift. And a fine bird it was, my dear."

"Wasn't nothing," Jake mumbled.

"Yes it was, and you know it." Anna snapped in a mock scold. "You see, Mister, geese cost too much in the store, but Jake knows how much I love a nice plump goose for Christmas Eve dinner, so every year, he goes out and shoots one."

"That's . . . uh . . . nice," I stammered. But in the back of my mind I wasn't sure it was such a big deal. Lots of folk hunt their own geese.

"You don't get it, do you Mister?" Anna continued. "Jake works six days a week from seven to five. So what he does during the season is work from seven in the morning until nine at night on Thursday and Friday so he can get most of Saturday off.

"The hunting grounds are a good two hours drive away, and he needs to be there by dawn, so he leaves here around 3 A.M., drives to the preserve, then wades for about three or four miles to his special blind right in the middle of the flyway. Sometimes he has to keep that sort of schedule for a whole month so he can get me one."

I shook my head. "That seems like an awful lot of trouble."

"Not too much, Mister," Jake spoke up. "I gotta make sure I come home with that goose for Christmas—it's all she ever asks for, and my secret spot hasn't failed me yet."

All this time, Jo-Jo had been gazing into the fire. Now, he stood, and, from under the small Christmas tree, brought two packages. Only one was really a package—the other was an envelope. Anna took the envelope from her son, and, holding it in her lap, addressed the group.

"This year I've written a Christmas poem. I hope you like it. It's from me to you with all my love. I call it 'A Song in the Heart.' "

"She writes something every year," Jake explained with pride. "Keeps her up sort of late what with her job and all, but she likes doing it, and we love 'em, too. Sometimes she writes a story, sometimes a poem. We keep 'em in a scrapbook."

I really didn't know what to expect—"Roses are red/ Violets are blue/ I like Christmas/ How about you" or something equally trite, but it's not what I got.

Anna's voice was soothing and clear.

There's an old, old song of blessing
   in the heart
That holds the cherished melody
   of years.
It still resounds when unseen angels
   part
The clouds that hide the Christ
   with human fears.

In the night it stills the fretful
   little child,
Or wakes the laughter lost in
   lonely hearts.
It hides a song where songs have
   never smiled,
And to the humble, holiness
   imparts.

In this old, old song, forgotten
   friendships sing,
And dreams awake in treasure
   trove of Star.
The weary throngs their awesome
   silence bring
As Wise Men brought their rich
   gifts from afar.

Let the bells of earth and heaven
   ring together
With the glad tidings of the
   Saviour's birth;
For Righteousness and Peace have
   kissed each other:
God's Love is living Song of
   the Soul's worth.[1]

No one spoke for a while. Then Jo-Jo shuffled across to his folks in his peculiar bent-legged fashion and handed them the package he clutched tightly in his hands.

"Merry Chismas . . . again!" he said in a funny sort of way, and I didn't understand, but Jake and Anna smiled and slowly unwrapped the package.

It was a manger—no more than five- or six-inches long— unremarkable at first. But when I held it—they passed it over to be admired—I realized it had been carved from a single block of wood.

"This is beautiful, Jo-Jo," I said. "Just beautiful."

Jo-Jo didn't reply. He just grinned, obviously pleased by my reaction.

"It's really lovely," I continued. "Must have taken some time, huh? Hours, I bet."

"It takes him four months," Jake said quietly. "He begins late August every year. He finished up yesterday—has trouble holding the tools, and if he sits in one position too long, he gets real uncomfortable. Never does it exactly the same way twice. At least not yet, and he's been at it since he was seven."

"I'm not sure what you mean," I said.

"Look over the mantle, Mister. That'll help."

I don't know how I missed them. Standing on the mantle, stretched across its length, was a row of mangers. Some were carved, most nailed or glued, one of oak, one of pine; wide, narrow, large, small, each one a little different. I counted fifteen in all.

Then I finally caught on. Jo-Jo was retarded.

I started to speak, but Jake help up his hand. "Hang on a minute, Mister, there's more. Go ahead, son."

Jo-Jo began, with a smile on his face as though he were telling something he'd just heard for the first time. But, the story wasn't new.

"Joseph an' Mary went . . . to Bethlehem an' stayed in a barn . . . an' Mary had a baby . . . an' wrapped . . . him in a blanket . . . an' put him in a manger . . . an' the baby was Jesus."

And as the boy stumbled through the most moving rendition of the Christmas narrative I have ever heard, I swear that manger came to life. Not dancing or talking or anything weird, it just looked alive. The wood lost its harshness and took on a soft, even tender quality.

I know it was the flickering of the fire combined with my own weariness, but the little hand-carved feed box seemed to breathe as if it had a life of its own. Suddenly the manger, in all its graphic simplicity, symbolized what Christmas should be:

a husband wearing himself out to insure his wife's craving for goose would be satisfied.

a mother sitting by the fire into the wee hours of the morning, losing precious sleep while composing a poem for those she loves.

a child, who would forever remain a child, lovingly

laboring on a miniature manger because the Prince of Peace needed a place to lay his head.

a family opening their home to a stranger on a night almost universally reserved exclusively for relatives, and stretching a meal for three to feed four, not out of pride, but because of a genuine respect for their duty to hospitality.

a simple, unembellished celebration of caring for and helping one another, friends and strangers alike, gathered around the rude bed that sheltered a king whose only royal command was "love one another."

We were all still looking at the manger when Jo-Jo began again, maybe because it was all he knew, maybe because it was all he thought important.

". . . wrapped him . . . in a blanket an' put him . . . in a manger an' the baby was Jesus."

* * * * *

I pulled into my driveway a little after noon the next day. The roads wore a deep jacket of snow, but Jake Trimble's four-wheel-drive had made steady if not speedy headway.

"Just drop it off next time through, Mister," Jake had said. "Right now you need it more than we do."

It was good to see the assembled clan, and they were glad I'd made it home safely. They even waited lunch for me. After hugs and kisses, handshakes and backslaps, they all trooped into the dining room while I went to wash up.

Coming through the den on my way back into the dining room, where another "feast to end all feasts" awaited, I stopped by the fireplace, removed my down jacket, and reached into the deep pocket. I took out the Trimble's Christmas gift to me: the man-child's copy of the Godchild's throne.

With a smile, I put Jo-Jo's sixteenth manger on my mantle. And it's been there ever since.

The Communion That Almost Wasn't

*A*s he stood for the second hymn of the Christmas Eve Communion service, Larson Spearman searched desperately for an excuse. *Maybe I could act sick—double up and stagger out. Better yet, faint. Yeah, just keel over, take a dive. Naw, that won't work. One of these hotshot doctors'll see through it and then I'll really be in trouble. It'll be all over.*

But so what? So what if it were over? He wanted it to end. He longed, craved, lusted for a finale. Wasn't that precisely the problem?

He felt tired, out of touch, empty. And not without reason. Twenty-five years of ordination could wear anyone down.

Larson had endured twenty-five years of forty-eight-hour-a-day availability, rushing out morning, noon, and night to deal with crises real and imagined. He had survived twenty-five years of "Pastor, I enjoyed the sermon," from folks who hadn't been listening; twenty-five years of apologizing for having opinions; a quarter of a century of hiding the fact that he was a human being—a fallible, weak, frightened-out-of-his-wits-by-failure human being.

Though he'd been cognizant of the sentiments and resentments for some time, today they threatened to overwhelm him. And Larson knew why: Communion—the gathering around the table of blessing, supposedly the highest experience of worship, was this evening for Larson only an exacerbation of his anger.

Twenty-five years of ministry and two hundred Communion services. Could it be? Yes, he'd checked earlier. It was two hundred exactly. Since beginning as a sparkling-eyed fledgling in his first pastorate, he'd carefully recorded every time he'd administered the sacrament. The list went on for pages, the older sheets now crumpled and soft with the handling of years. Two hundred Communions, averaging eight per year—pretty high for a man of his denomination—but, after all, he stood in great demand.

"Your services are so meaningful," they cooed.

"I feel so much a part."

They did. He didn't. Two-hundred ecclesiastical tea parties, a refreshment break to shatter the monotony of the routine. It hadn't always been this way, but the thrill he'd once felt, the stimulation generated by rite and rubric, slowly and inexorably found itself replaced by a numbing detachment. As if outside his own body, Larson now often watched himself lead the service. He watched with ponderous disinterest: the bread and the cup, the body and the blood, tidbits of crackly wafer slung to a congregation like saltines to so many birds, chased with shot glasses of Welch's finest. The service, no longer a festival, was merely a quarterly oiling of the ecclesiastical machinery. It was not an experience as much as an exercise—calisthenics for the soul. It was no longer an occasion for joy, but an orgy of precision: "Preacher, I know you'll never get all the elders to make square, military corners—particularly those young ones—but couldn't you at least make 'em all wear navy blue suits?"

Two hundred Communions, this one supposedly a time for special cheer. But the festive spirits bypassed Larson's heart.

* * * * *

The congregation lurched into the second stanza of the carol—not an overly familiar one—a fact sure to elicit heaps of comment: "Where'd you dig that one up?" "Hey, why can't we sing something we know, *especially* at Christmas?" "Larson, you know I've got a dust allergy—don't drag out those moldy old tunes."

Larson grimaced at the thought of the barrage he'd endure following worship and slowly scanned the congregation. For all the world he wished that he could pass this Christmas Eve in the solitude of his study, but his flock awaited:

Darletta Finch, possessor of a frighteningly precise coiffure, chaired the furnishings committee with snobbish vengeance. Lately she'd led the Great Drape Crusade. "Larson, I don't care how much sewing the woman does on her own, I don't care she majored in home economics, and I don't care if she's volunteered, she can't possibly do as good a job as someone from outside the church. You know, a professional. We need parlor drapes done by an expert. I won't have anything but custom-tailored drapes in my home and I will not accept something less in my church."

Darletta carried the day, as usual, streamrolling everything and everyone in her path. The professionally made parlor curtains hung as a monument to her persistence, and the home economics major transferred her membership to the church across the street.

Old George stood in his usual place. He never missed a Sunday. Old George never missed a session meeting, either, though he never said anything. Larson couldn't even remember if Old George voted. In twelve years Larson had never heard anything out of Old George much more than "hello," "good-bye," and an occasional comment on the relative merits of the various desserts offered at church suppers. "Stay away from the German chocolate cake, Parson. It's tough as an old shoe."

Somewhere out there lurked Miss X—at least the handwriting indicated a woman. Although Larson didn't know her identity, and probably never would, he heard from Miss X regularly. He usually found her unsigned notes slipped under his door when he arrived at his study on Mondays. "Your sermon did nothing for me today." "Since you are no longer interested in visiting, perhaps you should consider a change in pastorate." "The organ is far too loud." "Why don't you pray for more spiritual things?" Wonderful friend, Miss X.

Elliott Fitzhue was Larson's thorn in the flesh. Against everything, as up-to-date as an Edsel, Elliott personally orchestrated the opposition to the building campaign. Oh, he hadn't attracted too many supporters—no more than five to seven percent of the congregation, but their howls of indignation were so vehement that the session seriously considered delaying any action until "the climate proves more favorable." Elliott hadn't stopped the fund drive, but he certainly had muddied the waters.

*   *   *   *   *

Third stanza. According to his long-established custom, now simply a mechanical habit, Larson sunk into the bishop's chair next to the table, with his head in his hands. But prayer eluded him. Instead, other faces jumped into view:

Bob Seals, a common laborer, who had pledged thirty percent of his meager income to the new building.

Anne Farnsworth, a teenager who was rapidly turning the corner from self-doubt to self-worth, dropping by every other Wednesday, like clockwork, just for a hug and a hello.

Jean Dykstra, married one day, widowed the next; her husband, a bright young surgeon, killed by a fool too late for work to watch either the speed limit or the joggers.

And Larson remembered Tony Anderson sitting in the pew with his five scrubbed and polite children.

Tony showed up every Sunday, rain or shine, hot or cold, intent on every word despite having spent half the previous night looking for his wife and the other half bailing her out and sobering her up.

Then the first series of faces appeared to him again, but this time they seemed softer, more vulnerable:

He saw Darletta clutching his hand as they both prayed over the freshly dug grave of her spouse of forty-three years.

Old George, still silent, was doing the only thing at which he excelled—being there. Miss X, unidentified and probably very lonely, was focusing on him the agony of some unseen affliction that he'd been too busy or too blind to see. He saw Elliott Fitzhue hustling a herd of kids from the children's home into this year's version of the circus, with tickets, popcorn, programs, cotton candy, and at least one souvenir per child all at Elliot's expense.

Visage after visage rolled in front of him, familiar, vague, good, bad, friend, antagonist, but each with needs, each with pain, each with gifts, each with faults.

Then he saw his own face—sterner than he liked to imagine it—his eyes, once the windows to a warm, compassionate heart, now slightly glazed with the cataract of indifference; his lips set in a semi-petrified grimace, neither smile nor sneer, yet both at the same time.

And he could hear his own voice resonating the Communion passage from First Corinthians:

Whoever, therefore, eats the bread or drinks the cup in an unworthy manner will be guilty of profaning the body and blood of the Lord. Let a man examine himself, and so eat of the bread and drink of the cup.[2]

Examine himself, not critique others. Today of all days. Even the most benevolent appraisal disclosed the faults and fissures in Larson's character as it did in the personalities of everyone else. Closing his prayer, Larson remembered the story of what the old Scottish preacher said to the woman who hesitated to drink from the cup: "Take it, madam. It is for sinners. It is for you."

* * * * *

The fourth stanza swelled, and Larson stood weaving his rich tenor with the other voices. Only this time he paid attention to the words.

And our eyes at last shall see Him,
Through His own redeeming love;
For that child so dear and gentle
Is our Lord in heaven above,
And He leads His children on
To the place where He is gone.[3]

As the organ rang and the voices blended, Larson joined the great army of the wounded—God's people—who trudge, warts and all, with weary, sometimes faltering steps toward the table to touch, taste, and be filled with the presence and peace of Christ promised in the sacrament.

The carol ended. The congregation sat. The associate pastor prayed.

Then, Larson—pastor, sinner, recipient of grace, not healed but healing, not spotless but forgiven—stood behind the table and broke the bread.

Jerry Pender's Christmas Eve

*U*ntil now Jerry Pender had always enjoyed Christmas. Usually his excitement started building as Thanksgiving rolled by and the Yule season began. But this year he felt flat. And he knew why.

His wife noticed it, too. At first she wasn't going to say anything. Maybe work was tough. The promotion seemed great, but the additional responsibilities, the problems always associated with a move to a different town, and all those new people to meet weighed on him.

But Jerry had always handled challenges pretty well, so after a while she knew the job had nothing to do with his pre-Christmas funk.

Finally she'd had it. "Jerry, what's the matter with you? Ever since Thanksgiving you've been wandering around here like you've lost your best friend. What in the world is bothering you?"

Jerry hesitated a moment, feigning reluctance to speak, but he had neither the time nor the inclination to play the "let's weasel out what's bothering Jerry" game, so he let it go.

"Well, honey, in some ways I have—lost my best friend, I mean. Maybe I'm making too big a deal out of it, but it's gotten to be sort of special. I mean, I've done it every year for as long as I can remember, and now I feel sort of use-less—out of place or something. Don't you see, Paula? No one's asked me to sing."

She nodded. Jerry had been in choirs since before she'd known him. He wanted to join the one here, and he was a good enough sight reader to pick up whatever they were singing, but the two of them had arrived only six weeks ago and Jerry was still helping straighten out the house and get things ironed out at work. One Wednesday evening he'd gotten as far as the church driveway when his beeper went off and he had to rush over to the office to deal with some emergency.

Paula knew Jerry wasn't sulking. He wasn't the temperamental type. He just loved his music. And why shouldn't he?

She could remember Jerry's face blackened for the part of Balthazar, king of Ethiopia, for a performance of Menotti's *Amahl and the Night Visitors.* His eyes gleamed as he bent and sang to the awestruck little cripple, "I live in a big marble palace full of black panthers and white doves." She remembered the majestic cadences of Handel's baritone opus from *Messiah:* "But who may abide the day of his coming. . . ." And her favorite—Jerry standing in the upper reaches of the balcony, booming out "Go tell it on the mountain" to a darkened sanctuary.

The man was gifted. Pretty soon the question changed from "Jerry, will you sing this Christmas?" to "What do you have planned for this year?" Every year people seemed genuinely moved by Jerry's talent and his sharing of it. But this year no one had asked him to sing.

Nothing could be done. The church's Advent and Christmas music had long been in preparation, and to interrupt the scheme would have been presumptuous, not to mention impossible. So Jerry made the best of it. Still, though he put forth every effort to participate in seasonal functions, even hosting a party for their newly found friends, she could tell his heart just wasn't quite in it.

The day before Christmas came and went without incident. Jerry returned early from work. No one was getting anything done at the office, and they'd been pleased when Jerry sent them all home. So the two of them spent the late afternoon doing some last-minute shopping and preparing for the arrival of family members the next day.

But as the time to go to church drew near, Jerry grew more and more agitated. No, "agitated" isn't the right word, this was more like nervousness. Jerry fidgeted like a star running back whom the doctors won't allow to play, but who suits up in uniform and full pads anyway and hovers next to the coach snapping, unsnapping, and re-snapping his chin strap in hope he'll get sent in but knowing he's benched.

Seven-thirty finally came and Jerry bolted for the door, car keys in hand.

Paula stopped him cold. "Jerry Pender, where do you think you're going?"

"To church, of course. It's Christmas Eve."

"Jerry," Paula's voice snapped in peevish sympathy, "We have gone to church together every Christmas Eve for the last twenty-four years. For the last twenty-four years I've gone with you an hour-and-a-half early so you could be on time for rehearsal. I've sat in empty, dark, sometimes cold sanctuaries while you, 'fa, la, la'd' in the choir room. But not tonight!

"I love Christmas Eve. I love Christmas Eve services. I don't even know what they do here on Christmas Eve, and I know I'll love it. But we're not going now. The service isn't until nine. You don't have to be early.

"In fact, you're not going at all. You'll drive me crazy. You don't know how to act in church, not unless you're in the choir. Remember last week? You stood up with the choir when they got ready for the anthem. We sit in the middle of the sanctuary, and you stood up. You hummed all the responses—you hummed that last amen so loud that the people next to us stared.

"No sir, mister, I'm going to church, but you can go some-place else."

* * * * *

That's how he ended up at The Haven. The one nonwork activity he'd been able to squeeze in was visiting the children's home on behalf of his civic club. He was only required to go once every two weeks, but he dropped in a couple of times a week, usually during lunch, because The Haven was close to the office.

Jerry didn't see himself as the good Samaritan type, but it made him feel better to help the kids. They really didn't have much, and they needed all the help they could get.

"Hey Jerry," called Homer Murphy, popping Jerry's bubble of thought. "Jerry, boy, am I glad to see you. We've got a problem. Come on."

As he hustled down the hall behind the squatty director, Jerry listened intently.

"Mikey Souffers seems pretty sick, Jerry. I've never seen anything like it. At first I thought it was a bad cold or something, maybe even strep 'cause Mikey's had some trouble swallowing, but all of a sudden it's gotten worse. I think he may need to go to the hospital.

"I can't leave, 'cause I'm the only staff here right now. The rest went to look at the lights. Come on, he's in here."

Mikey hunched over the edge of his bed, gasping for air. His labored breathing sounded a little like the bark of a seal—harsh, raspy, and very strained. Saliva dripped from his open mouth. His three roommates cowered in the corner, reluctant to leave their friend, but afraid to get too close.

Jerry took one look and headed back down the hall.

* * * * *

The doctor's voice on the phone was crisp and precise. "From the symptoms you describe, Mister Pender, it sounds like the child has epiglottitis. That's a bacterial inflammation of the epiglottis. Could be complicated by tracheitis, bronchitis, or some other upper respiratory problem. He needs to come to the hospital right now, into the operating room for a procedure called an 'endotracheal intubation.' We insert a little. . . ."

"Whoa, Doc, hold it! You're talking treatment, and I don't even know what he's got. Go over it again."

"I'm sorry, Mr. Pender. Okay. You know the little flap of tissue that covers the trachea—the windpipe?—when you swallow—you know, so food doesn't end up in your lungs?"

"Uh huh."

"Well, it's usually in the open position so that the air can flow when you breathe. If I'm right, the little trap door—the epiglottis—has become infected. It's so badly swollen it's affecting the airflow. Mikey can't breathe very well. That's why he's wheezing.

"It also hurts to swallow, so much he really can't swallow, and that's why he's drooling. When he comes in, assuming my diagnosis is correct, I'm going to insert a little tube into his windpipe, and that'll help him breathe better until the infection responds to antibiotics."

"Okay, Doc. Sounds good. I'll stay with him 'til the ambulance gets here."

"No!" The doctor spoke with such force that Jerry almost dropped the phone. "Don't call an ambulance. Listen very carefully. You can't let the child become excited. He's scared enough as it is because he can't breathe. The lights and siren and smells and unfamiliar people in the ambulance will terrify him. He'll panic. If he gets too scared, the airway will spasm and close. He'll suffocate to death before he gets here.

"You've got to keep him calm. You have to bring him yourself."

* * * * *

It took a while for the car's heater to warm up, but even after the interior was toasty, Jerry held Mikey close. Cradling the child while he drove certainly wasn't the safest thing, but Jerry wasn't going to let go now. Snow started falling again, but this time its usual frolicking dance had something of a menacing quality to it. There wouldn't be any work crews tonight. The trip to St. Joseph's might take a while.

Jerry stole a quick glance at his cargo. Mikey's large, deep-set eyes had a trapped animal quality to them. They darted

from Jerry around the car as if looking for a way out. The strident breathing, scratching with the same quality of a fingernail dragging its creaky way across a blackboard, continued.

The longer they drove, the more frantic the eye movements became and the louder the breathing.

Away in a manger, no crib for a bed,
The little Lord Jesus lay down His sweet head.

When Jerry started, the tone was probably a little shaky—certainly not concert quality—but now wasn't a time to blast. Jerry kept reminding himself to take it easy. This was no performance. At least, not like he'd ever had before.

The stars in the bright sky looked down where He lay,
The little Lord Jesus, asleep on the hay.
The cattle are lowing, the poor baby wakes.
But little Lord Jesus, no crying He makes.

The longer Jerry sang, the calmer Mikey became. The eye movements slowed, and finally the little boy's dark eyes locked in a penetrating gaze on Jerry's face.

I love Thee, Lord Jesus! Look down from the sky,
And stay by my cradle 'til morning is nigh.
Be near me, Lord Jesus! I ask Thee to stay
Close by me forever, and love me, I pray.

The breathing—still scratchy and a little raspy but less labored—came at a slower, more deliberate rate. Jerry kept on driving.

Bless all the dear children in Thy tender care,
And fit us for heaven, to live with Thee there.

* * * * *

The operating room, with its unyielding, somewhat frosty sterility of bright lights, gleaming instruments, and barren walls presented a stark contrast. The surgeon, anesthesiologist, and two nurses clustered around the table like four

green-cowled ghosts of Christmases yet to come. The frigid-
ity of the environs was balanced against the warmth of the
child Jerry clutched in his arms.

Jerry walked to the head of the table as per the surgeon's
instructions.

"No reason to move him now, Mr. Pender, he's used to
you. We'll anesthetize him while you hold him. Don't worry
about scrubbing. It'll be okay."

So Jerry continued to hum his lullaby, the tune probably
inaudible to the busy surgical team, but Jerry knew Mikey
could feel the vibrations of the melody because the child
snuggled closer.

Mikey took the gas without any problem, his eyes rolling
upward, his lids slamming shut with a noiseless snap. Jerry
didn't want to give him up, but he knew he'd done all he
could. So he laid his sleeping little friend on the operating
table, and backed out the swinging door.

* * * * *

Jerry stayed until Mikey came out of recovery and was in
a room. The child couldn't talk because of the tube in his
throat, but he did smile, and when Jerry leaned over to say
good-night, the little fellow hugged him.

Tired as he was, Jerry headed for the parking lot with a
new spring in his step.

There hadn't been any accompaniment, and the audience
had been very limited. The tune was nothing more than a
child's carol. But the music of the season had never been
quite so alive.

Jerry Pender had gotten his chance to sing after all.

The Lights of Kensington Corner

*T*hey said he was crazy, the old man who lived on the hill. The claim probably held some justification. After all, he did keep his house decorated for Christmas all year. No one really knew why, but legends abounded.

The most popular tale concerned the old man's wife. She died quite unexpectedly on Christmas Eve some time ago, back before the old man was old. He hasn't come out since, except to replace a burned-out bulb, change a strand of lights, or add something new to his electronic menagerie. When he actually ventured from his house, he only did so at night, which added even more fuel to the fires of suspicion concerning his mental stability. Keeping the decorations up must have been his idea of a memorial, or maybe he was waiting for his wife to come home, or maybe his mind was frozen in time.

But the old man's alleged insanity didn't keep the good citizens of Kensington Corner away. They came every year on Christmas Eve to see the lights on the crazy old man's house. No one remembered how the viewing started, but it had become more of a tradition than anyone probably realized.

The first few folk arrived at the top of the hill about 10:30, with plenty of time to spare since the old codger never

turned anything on until precisely 11:00 P.M. every year. After a while the trickle of people turned into a steady stream, with some arriving on foot, some in cars, a few on bikes, and a number of groups of rowdy youngsters in church buses.

Moms and dads came with their broods, each family there for a different reason. Some parents were rewarding good behavior; some were simply keeping the kids out of the house and away from the beckon of the brightly-wrapped presents; some were probably just trying to wear the little people out so that everyone could get some sleep before the big day.

Here and there young couples stood cuddling infants just as their parents had held them years before. The children, large and small, presented quite a sight. Most were dressed in shiny shoes (they'd obviously been to church) and bundled in warm coats with stocking caps pulled low over brow and ears, their rosy cheeks and eyes shining with the brightness uniquely a child's at Christmas. The older kids fidgeted or wandered or ran. A few stayed close to their parents. The very young slept, oblivious to the excitement and not at all impressed that Santa would soon visit.

Yet some of the youngsters weren't with parents at all, and the majority of the inhabitants of Kensington Corner avoided the group of young street toughs perched like so many prepubescent vultures on their habitual roost atop the old man's brick wall. In the middle of the adolescent riff-raff slumped ring leaders Billy and Bobby Holloway.

Bad kids of worse parents, Billy and Bobby managed to stay in trouble. Whenever anything started—cigarette smoking in the school restrooms, egg-throwing incidents, tasteless graffiti on the walls of city hall—the police ran Billy and Bobby in on suspicion, and despite their protests of innocence, everyone knew the Holloways were behind it. Besides, if Billy and Bobby were ever prosecuted for something they didn't do, it would only serve as just punishment for something they'd undoubtedly gotten away with earlier.

As the minutes dragged on the crowd got bigger. Everyone

murmured when Francey Velour slinked up the walk—not because her arrival was a surprise, but because everyone always murmured when Francey showed up. She didn't work, she had no known source of income. Everyone knew her family was broke, too, but Francey always dressed in stylish—not to mention revealing—costumes. Bracelets jingled on her wrists and her diamond ring seemed to flash even in the dark. What a rock!! Some folks swore it was fake, but most preferred to accept its authenticity because such supposition allowed them to engage in protracted, eyebrow-raised speculation as to how she got it.

Once the grounds were full and the house completely surrounded, Elwood Starling took over. For as long as anyone could remember, Elwood had served as the self-appointed master of ceremonies for the Christmas Eve house-lighting event. He weaved through the crowd, the aroma of four-dollar-a-gallon wine clinging to him like a parasitic vine.

Mothers shielded their children, Billy and Bobby led the jeers, the Right Reverend Norman Van Vleet scowled his most condescending holier-than-thou scowl and "tsk, tsked" as loudly as anyone can "tsk," but Elwood would not be denied his day in the sun—even if it was at night.

"Don't worry folksch," Elwood belched, "the lightsch will be on momenn . . . momenn . . . in a little bit. Hey, fool, don't push, there's little kiddiesch present. Don't crowd, people, everyone will be able to shee. Yo! There's room over there for two or three, yeah, that's it. Everybody'll have a goo' time. Meeery Christmas!"

On he staggered, pausing every so often at intervals determined by his infrequent moments of lucidity, delivering his little speech to a predominantly tolerant audience. Old, bagged Elwood was as much a part of Christmas Eve as anything else.

At exactly 10:58 P.M., Mrs. G. Winslow Prescott arrived in her limousine. She came every year, not due to any interest in the trite little folk custom, but to distribute candy and trinkets to, as she called them, "the poor unfortunate urchins." But woe to the "urchin" unfortunate enough to brush up against Mrs. G. Winslow Prescott's sleek, silver and black Rolls Royce, or (God forbid!) Mrs. G. Winslow Prescott herself, for there would descend upon the offending miscreant a life-threatening scowl conveying all sorts of mayhem and violence. Besides, if you touched the old bat, you didn't get any Santa Claus suckers.

Mrs. G. Winslow Prescott showed up every year at 10:58 P.M. because she hated to be kept waiting. Perhaps she assumed if she were fifteen minutes late, the lighting ceremony would be delayed until she arrived. If, indeed, she harbored any such conviction, she was never foolish enough to put it to the test. It never occurred to her the old man neither knew nor cared if Mrs. Winslow Prescott came at all.

But maybe he did, because the instant Mrs. P. set foot inside the gate, as if by cue, the lights came on, and in the shower of brilliance the crowd first gasped and then applauded. They'd never applauded before. Most usually grinned and giggled, a few nodded approvingly, even fewer occasionally let out a Yuletide whoop, but no one had ever applauded the demented old gentleman's handiwork. But this was fantastic!

Never had the old man's house been so elaborately decorated. The entire dwelling was outlined in flashing red and white pinlights, the boxwoods, too. At a glance the house looked like a giant peppermint mountain. Each first-floor window had been trimmed in a different color and, in the respective windows stood candles of a matching hue, complete with flicker-flame bulbs. Electric oscillations of green, gold, magenta, and turquoise jitterbugged across the panes to the delight of everyone in the yard.

The second story was wondrous to behold. Three intertwined strands of vivid green lights figure-eighted the upstairs windows, giving them the appearance of being encased in a garland of evergreen. A special Christmas scene graced every casement.

In the first window, a brilliant block-lettered "Ho-Ho-

Ho" lit up one-two-three, one-two-three, inspiring some of the children to begin a chant in time to the flashes.

A jolly snowman, complete with top hat and pipe, pulsated at opening number two, standing small, medium, large, small, medium, large, over and over again.

The third featured a pair of Christmas bells cling-clanging in silent sequence, appearing first at the right, then at the left, back and forth.

"Merry Christmas" in green neon script blazed in the fourth window as tiny red bulbs danced around the edges of the message.

High atop the house, perched in a brilliantly illuminated sleigh, sat Old Saint Nick himself. Out in front, eight tiny reindeer, legs skittering back and forth, streaked motionless across the rooftop. From out of Santa's bag peeked a floppy-eared puppy, and those with good eyesight could barely discern his eager little tail wagging against the night sky.

All in all the lights gave the house the appearance of a stationary fireworks display exploding noiselessly against a backdrop of black.

And then suddenly the lights went out.

This never happened before. Usually the lights burned until the wee hours of the morning, then disappeared until next Christmas Eve. But here, at only 11:15 P.M., the lights were off.

At first everyone assumed some sort of momentary power failure, but after five minutes of semi-patient waiting, it became apparent that the extravaganza had ended. So they all began to leave, sauntering back the way they had come, some laughing and chattering, others mumbling and grumbling, "Best show ever and it ended early—that's what I call bad luck."

Mrs. G. Winslow Prescott huffed back toward the Rolls, flicking baubles and pieces of candy to her adoring subjects as she departed. Billy and Bobby Holloway slithered off the wall and skulked around, eyes peeled for anyone not holding onto a purse tightly enough. Elwood reached toward the flask in his inside coat pocket.

"Look!" They all froze in their tracks and turned to see a little boy pointing into the air. "Look up there," he shouted, "over the house!" They all looked.

Up in the sky, some twenty or thirty feet above the old man's roof, burned a single white star. Even though everyone knew it had to be sitting on a long pole, the solitary beacon seemed suspended in midair. Gazing at it, the people slowly shuffled back toward the house. Silence prevailed as each individual stood alone with his or her own thoughts, lost in transfixed reverence.

No one knows who started it, but the voice was firm and clear.

O little Town of Bethlehem, How still we see thee lie! Above thy deep and dreamless sleep The silent stars go by;

One by one all joined in. One by one they picked up the prayerful song—Mrs. G. Winslow Prescott's shaky warble, the Rev. Van Vleet's tin-earred monotone, old Elwood's alcohol-scented slur.

Yet in thy dark streets shineth The everlasting Light: The hopes and fears of all the years Are met in thee tonight.

And as they sang, some strange things happened. Mrs. G. Winslow Prescott knelt on the ground and extended her arms to a gaggle of ill-clad little boys. At first they just looked at her, bewildered, but the arms remained outstretched, and soon the youngsters nestled warmly in the folds of the elderly woman's fur coat.

How silently, how silently, The wondrous gift is given! So God imparts to human hearts The blessings of His heaven.

While the boys snuggled closer, Mrs. P. laid her clutch bag on the ground beside her, but Billy Holloway, standing nearby, was too busy singing even to notice.

Elwood, eyes riveted on the light, reached for his flask and quietly poured the contents on the ground.

No ear may hear His coming, But in this world of sin, Where meek souls will receive Him still, The dear Christ enters in.

With tears streaming down her made-up cheeks, Francey Velour stood off by herself. She'd been right at home with the gaudy decorations, but the frightening simplicity of the star made her uncomfortable. She stood alone until the Right Reverend Norman Van Vleet gently touched her hand and drew her into the larger crowd.

The human circle ringed the house, all voices singing together. The Christmas decorations had been extinguished, but the light of Christmas blazed in everyone's heart.

O holy Child of Bethlehem! Descend to us, we pray; Cast out our sin and enter in, Be born in us today.

Surely they all knew the song would eventually end, that they'd drop hands, go their separate routes, and probably return to the ways they'd always done things. But for one Christmas Eve, gathered under the light of a star if only for an instant, the citizens of Kensington Corner fulfilled the promise of peace on earth and good will to all.

We hear the Christmas angels The great glad tidings tell; O come to us, abide with us, Our Lord Emmanuel!

They said he was crazy, the old man who lived on the hill, but I'm not so sure.

One Christmas Eve

*T*he echoes of the clock's chimes slowly faded away, leaving only the timepiece's steady ticking and the muffled sound of voices from the living room. Eleven P.M.— Christmas Day lurked only an hour away.

From his place on the couch, he surveyed the dimly lit den. "Same as always," he muttered, and a matter-of-fact grin flashed across his face.

The tree stood in its old familiar spot, bright as ever. The twinkling lights bouncing off tinsel garland and aluminum foil icicles painted kaleidoscopic pictures on the ceiling. Packages of every imaginable description surrounded the evergreen. Some sported elaborately patterned paper and huge bows. Simple brown boxes indicated the ones that had come by mail. In the back, he could see the one wrapped in newspaper—same as every year. His brother always bought a nice gift, but frugality would not allow him to fritter away money on gift wrapping.

Along the length of the mantle, the stockings hung in limp expectation. There weren't as many as there once were (this year the grandparents stayed home and they didn't have a dog), but for the most part, they were the same as always. His, marked "Daddy," dangled along with the rest. Years ago he'd suspected his was smaller than everyone else's, but

Saint Nick somehow always managed to fill it to overflowing.

From its perch on the far wall, the Santa Claus mailbag peered out over the room as it had every year for as long as he could remember. Once again the red and white pouch sagged with the weight of holiday greetings.

Everything occupied its usual place; it was Christmas like always. Then his eye caught something in the far corner of the room. In the darkness he could just make out the family's old nativity scene on a small table nestled, almost hidden, in the corner.

It sat off by itself—the same one he'd had as a child. At one time the set had been a beautiful, colorful recreation of Bethlehem's most famous evening. Now Mary's dress, originally a shimmering blue, appeared the color of lint. The palm trees on either side of the dilapidated stable stood palmless—naked little green pipe cleaners with clay bases. The infant Jesus perched precariously in a three-sided manger. The angel of the Lord, bent trumpet in hand, stood atop the stable, her broken wings evidence of a youthful experiment in aerodynamics.

The crèche rested on what once had been a brillant piece of crimson velvet. The passage of years and the batter of constant use had left it little more than a shiny red rag.

"I wonder why it's over there?" he mumbled. How times had changed. He could remember himself, thirty-five or forty years younger, kneeling in front of the little stable, the baby Jesus cradled gently in his hands. As the youngest in the family, he was awarded the honor of putting the Child in the manger on Christmas Eve. Every year he lowered the small figure into the tiny wooden bed and said, "Happy Birthday, Jesus." Then the family sang "Silent Night" together.

They invented the little ceremony themselves, and the tradition continued year after year. Even during his college days, when cynicism ran rampant, he secretly took great pride in the fact that he put Jesus in the manger.

Some time ago he and his wife had considered trying the

same thing with the children, but the idea never got off the ground. They had too much to do on Christmas Eve, too many other decorations to put up. Besides, they needed to get everything squared away and the kids off to bed to await Santa—no time for sentimental rituals.

He started to turn on the television, but the flicker of a candle made him turn his head. A merry little half-melted snowman struggled to add light to the den. As he stared at it he remembered another candle, one from long ago—this one tall, slender, and gleaming white.

Another of his privileges as the youngest had been to light the Christ candle in the Advent wreath. His family had always made a wreath and used it every day during the four weeks prior to Christmas as part of morning devotions. On Christmas Day, just before the family made their way into the den, he lit the white candle while his brothers and sisters recited the familiar words from Luke:

> And she gave birth to her first-born son and wrapped him in swaddling cloths, and laid him in a manger. . . .[4]

Then, carrying the candle, he led the excited little procession into the treasure room, and placed the taper on the table next to the stable before running over to his corner to investigate.

There was no Christ candle this year; there hadn't been one for a long time. They'd decided not to burden the children with too much stuff 'n nonsense on Christmas morning; it only slowed things down.

If they didn't move steadily through the opening of the presents, the banquet was delayed. Late meals made Mom irritable because she spent a lot of time cooking and hated to serve cold food. Tardy meals meant Mom grumped around all day and made life miserable for everyone. Once she got mad, she hassled him about watching the ballgame and that teed him off. A chain reaction of anger—all because of a little religious hoopla.

Besides, he'd already gone to church—went every Christmas Eve as a matter of fact. "Dragged" was a little more accurate because he hated spending what little free time he had hanging around the church. But for some reason, everyone really felt that you had to go to church "or it just isn't Christmas."

At least this year they hadn't done one of those insipid tableau things where everyone runs around in bathrobes and fake beards.

Then he remembered his own experience as a high school student dressed in the flowing robe his mother had made, with the burnoose draped over his head and shoulders. Frozen, hands in front of his face to shield his eyes from the spotlight-induced glare of the heavenly messenger (always portrayed by the tallest girl in the senior class), he'd listened to the narration:

> Fear not: for, behold, I bring you good tidings of great joy, which shall be to all people. For unto you is born this day in the city of David a Saviour, which is Christ the Lord.[5]

He had played the role of shepherd for three straight years. Oh, he'd had chances to do other things—even narrate from the pulpit—but something about watching the transformation of the string-bean girl into the stately, radiantly clad angel, something about the thundering simplicity of the announcement, something about the lights and the mood and the other boys' amazed faces really filled him with awe.

Every year he'd actually owned a sense of what it must have been like on the hill outside Bethlehem on the first Christmas Eve.

Thinking about those days of innocence and faith gave him a tingle of excitement. He simultaneously felt a twinge of regret as he considered how his family had missed out because he and his wife had been unwilling to encourage participation in church activities.

The sound of the kids in the living room interrupted his revelry. They'd been chatting in there since coming home

from the service, but now their voices were joined in song. All five sang well, and he thought how fortunate they were to have inherited their mother's musical talent.

He could hear them quite clearly singing "Joy to the World."

Suddenly it dawned on him that they had learned in spite of him. They'd done it on their own, without much guidance from the very ones who should have shown the way.

In his youth all the opportunities—to participate in the church pageant, to light the Christ candle, to lay the Child in the manger, to know the fullness and the joy of Christmas—had been open to him.

But his children grew up without those chances. Theirs had been Yules full of "Jingle Bells," but without the melody of "Silent Night." They had experienced Christmas Eve trips to church with begrudging and grumbling parents, Christmas mornings full of toys, games, and clothes, but devoid of any mention of the Babe of Bethlehem.

Their voices grew louder.

Somehow they had learned. Despite the damper with which he'd smothered the holiness of the day, his children had managed to discover the radiant light of the Christmas star.

He got up from the couch and headed towards the singing. With his hand on the knob, he paused. He had something to do.

Walking to the far corner, he lifted the small table and carried it to the center of the room. The brilliance of the tree bathed the tiny stable and its miniature occupants in a shower of radiance. He was almost to the hall again when he heard his wife behind him.

"Honey, who put this manger scene in the middle of all the Christmas stuff?"

"I did," he said quietly. "And it's about time."

The Gift

Snow continued to fall as the last shouts of "Merry Christmas!" faded into the night. In the distance they could hear the door of the van close, the motor sputter to life, and the vehicle pull away.

Mom closed the door. "That was nice, I don't think we've ever been caroled before."

Henry rubbed his ears with exaggerated anguish. "Maybe next time they'll sing on key."

"Don't be such a creep, Henry," Gretchen snapped. "Even if they didn't sound so hot, they looked like they were having a good time."

Mom broke in, "Yes, dear, they really do enjoy themselves. I remember going from house to house with them, singing in the van, laughing . . . telling stories. . . ." Her voice faltered.

"That sounds like fun," Gretchen continued. "I bet you and Dad really enjoyed. . . ." She broke off and looked around self-consciously.

"Way to go, big mouth," John growled in an angry whisper. Then in a gentle voice, "Don't worry about it, Mom. She didn't mean to upset you."

"It's all right, John . . . Gretchen . . . Henry. I'm fine. I have nothing but pleasant memories of the Christmasses your father and I shared. We were married twenty-one wonderful years. . . . But enough!! It's Christmas Eve. We've got lots of stuff to do. Let's get busy!"

* * * * *

The tree stood majestically in the center of the room. It was a full twelve feet, but they always had tall trees. A smaller one would have been dwarfed in the cavernous, high-ceilinged den of the old house.

They'd moved into the house on baby John's first birthday. How exciting to move from a tiny apartment to a three-story mansion, or so it seemed. It was quite a change, and maybe a little risky, but Frank's practice had taken off, and with his money management acumen, paying for it never became a problem.

How ironic, she thought, *that one who dedicated most of his time to the preservation of life would die so swiftly.* They'd had so little time to prepare. It hardly seemed fair.

She shuddered with a sudden chill and inched closer to the fireplace in front of which they'd snuggled on the couch, surrounded by a regiment of boxes and crates, holding hands as she cuddled their tiny son on that first night so many years ago.

The house's seemingly endless transformation with patches, paint, and wallpaper crawled along. But when they finished, they felt proud. The den, the fireplace in particular, always remained the center of family activity. She smiled as she remembered all the family meetings. Whenever an important decision loomed or a problem arose, the family met in council around the fireplace. And always Frank was there with sage advice or penetrating questions or salient observations.

And always, on Christmas Eve, the celebration officially began from a gathering at the fireplace.

Christmas Eve! Good heavens—she'd forgotten! Snapping out of her private thoughts she saw the children encircling her, awaiting her instructions.

"What are you sitting around for, people?" she barked

with mirth-filled anger. "There's work to do. To the tree! to the tree!"

They spent the next hour decorating the towering pine. While John and Henry tested the bulbs, Gretchen strung popcorn as fast as she could. After the lights had been placed just so, the three began hanging the ornaments.

The inevitable annual arguments ensued. Gretchen thought she ought to place the angel at the top because . . . well, just because. And so what if Henry was the youngest? He got to do it every year.

John fussed because Gretchen and Henry insisted on flinging big globs of icicles on the tree instead of putting each individual aluminum strand in place one at a time.

Through it all Mom replenished the floundering cookie supply and brought in cup after cup of steaming, marshmallow-topped hot chocolate. Whenever things threatened to get out of hand, she stepped in as mediator, but for the most part, the arguments remained lighthearted and more for the sake of tradition than anything else. The tree trimming continued in a festive spirit.

Then the ritual of the gifts began. Everyone scurried away and returned loaded down with presents. From closet and shelf, from under bed and behind curtain, gifts appeared. It took a while to shove all the presents under the tree, but when the four family members once again sat in front of the fire, they stared in appreciation, temporarily mesmerized by the beauty of the pine rising up from its expansive nest of brightly wrapped packages.

Finally, as had become the custom, Mom walked to the tree, picked up a gift and read the name on the card. The little procession trooping from fireplace to tree to individual corner remained orderly for a while, but it accelerated quickly, everyone walking faster and faster, then almost running—the names now screamed above the stomping of feet and the shouts of glee as each recipient seized his or her newfound prize.

Before too long everyone was grabbing packages and calling out names, laughing as presents ended up in the wrong hands and had to be exchanged. The children alternated between worming their way under the low-hanging branches and dashing back to their corners to stack their gifts. John and Gretchen arranged theirs with meticulous precision. Henry simply piled one on top of the other until his treasure trove looked like the remnants of an avalanche.

Every so often, as they had during the tree trimming, one or another of the children stole a glance at the mantle where now hung only four stockings instead of five. And they'd clumsily brush away a tear with the hope no one else saw, because they didn't want to make this Christmas any more difficult.

Suddenly they were finished. No presents, no ornaments, nothing else to do. A heavy, oppressive, embarrassing silence stumbled across the floor. The time they'd all secretly dreaded had arrived.

Each year, when all else had been completed, and just prior to bed, Dad—always Dad—read the Christmas story from Luke. And every year, he somehow made it come to life. No matter how many times he'd read it before, each Christmas Eve the story seemed so fresh they could almost hear the angels singing and sense the terrifying wonder seizing the shepherds.

"I know what you're thinking," Mom said, interrupting the stillness to everyone's relief. "We read the Christmas story every year, and we will again tonight—just like always. But I have something else to read first.

"It's from your father. He wrote it the day before he died because he knew he wouldn't be with us. But he evidently had some thought he wanted to share, so he asked me if I'd read this. I'll try."

Reaching next to her, she picked up the family Bible—the one they'd read from every day at breakfast and every Christmas Eve. Opening it, she took out a gray envelope that the children immediately recognized as their father's stationery. Although her hands trembled slightly, her voice remained strong as she read.

My dearest family:

By now, all stands ready for the Great Day—the lights are strung, the tree is decorated, the arguments are settled, the cookies have been consumed and the gifts distributed. I suspect, however, the notes of the angelic chorus may sound a little flat tonight. You may have trouble believing there can be any "good tidings of great joy."

But as I consider all the Christmas Eves and Christmas Days we celebrated together, I am overwhelmed by the message that was delivered to the shepherds so long ago. Those simple herdsmen didn't receive a mere birth announcement. Instead, they witnessed the dawning of a new era—the age of the Lord Jesus.

Christmas in our home has always been a time of great happiness. And even as we rejoiced, we've endeavored to keep things in perspective. Our Christmases have always been celebrations of the Master's birth. But therein lies a problem, even if it seems small, because amid the gift giving, tree trimming, and hot chocolate sipping, we've put aside the fact that Jesus did not remain a child forever.

He grew, as we are told, "in wisdom and in stature, and in favor with God and man." Our Lord's birth proclaimed God's never-ending love for us. More importantly though, his life showed us the road we should follow and his death and resurrection taught us how to face our own end with the complete assurance we will live eternally with him.

It occurs to me that it is impossible for us to see the manger and miss the cross. We cannot recall the star without also remembering the empty tomb.

I do not want your Christmas Eve to become maudlin or sentimental. I have written this letter simply because I feel compelled to leave you something this year. Don't cry on my behalf, but know I am now with the One for whom the angels sang.

The only gift I can give you this year may be the

greatest gift I have ever given: the hope of every Christian. Dear family, rejoice! I would have you know I am spending Christmas with the Christ!!

All my love,
Dad

Mom folded the letter and slipped it back into the Bible, which she handed to John. Again silence held them, but this time its grip felt warmer—softer. It wasn't silence at all; it was peace.

Quietly, John began to read the Christmas story from Luke, and when he reached the familiar parts, first Mom, then Gretchen, then even Henry joined in.

And there were in the same country shepherds abiding in the field, keeping watch over their flock by night. And, lo, the angel of the Lord came upon them, and the glory of the Lord shown round about them: and they were sore afraid. And the angel said unto them, Fear not, for, behold, I bring you good tidings of great joy, which shall be to all people. For unto you is born this day . . . a Saviour, which is Christ the Lord. . . .

And suddenly there was with the angel a multitude of the heavenly host praising God, and saying, Glory to God in the highest. . . .[6]

They finished the story and one by one went off to bed. The fear of Christmas Day had vanished, and in its place rested a calm unlike any they'd ever known.

A Visit to Meadowbrook

*T*hey told me it was small, but this is ridiculous."
I looked around the sanctuary, trying to assess the situation. It was bad enough to endure Christmas away from home, but I had at least hoped for a decent worship service.

The room probably sat no more than seventy-five. The monotony of the unpainted cinder block walls yielded only long enough to accommodate an occasional, unadorned window.

Suddenly I missed the stained glass casements at my home church. With scenes from the New Testament on the right and scenes from the Old Testament on the left, the tinted panes diffused the light into an array of colors and mottled my own church's thousand-seat sanctuary like an artist's pallet. But this was hardly home.

Two large wall fans—one east, one west—clattered noisily. More boisterous than effective, they banged away oblivious to the intended reverence of the impending proceedings.

Unbelievable! Five o'clock in the afternoon on Christmas Eve and it's eighty degrees. But what else should I have expected in southern Florida? Aunt Matilda really wanted me to visit, and I really did owe her one. After all, she practically raised me. But honestly, Christmas in a swelter? Not exactly my cup of tea.

I renewed my perusal. Someone had obviously purchased all the chancel furniture from some mail-order ecclesiastical catalog and made the selections based more on economy than quality. The pulpit rose up awkwardly from center stage: a simple podium, lightweight, and consumately portable. Behind it stood an unupholstered straight-backed chair. Just off the stage, a smallish Communion table and baptismal font guarded the front stairs.

Over to the left a whitewashed piano balanced tenuously on three casters and a stack of plywood. On the wall, a hymnboard advertised the selections for the day.

Exactly when people started filing in I have no idea. I had been too intent on my estimation of the sparse facilities to notice. By the time I looked up, the room was over half full.

The more I examined the incoming congregation, the more out of place I felt. I could not find a single suit or tie among the men. Most of them wore trousers, work-type pants, not tailored slacks, and their shirts ranged from cotton to faded denim.

The cookie-cutter women all seemed middle-aged and were dressed in print smocks of varying colors; undistinguished in style and indeterminable in age. Their attempts to spruce up their outdated apparel with costume jewelry and loud hats fell short.

My silk dress grew increasingly uncomfortable, and I gave thanks I had left my fur at Matilda's. I realize wearing a mink in the heat seems silly, but it *was* Christmas Eve. Almost without thinking, I slid my sleeve down over my Rolex so no one would notice it.

I moved down the pew to allow a large man to sit. The fellow was a giant, well over six-and-a-half feet tall and at least two-hundred-and-eighty pounds. He jerked a nod, smiled bashfully, and mumbled "thanks." He was clean enough. In fact, he wore a sort of freshly scoured look, but he still gave the impression of having just come in from the south forty. His shoes—my children would have called them "clod hoppers"—were heavy and coarse. He wore dungarees and a work shirt with enough starch in it for a week's laundry. He had fastened the top button, and although it obviously made him uncomfortable, he steadfastly refused to unbutton it. Periodically he ran a finger around his collar and strained his neck as if trying to escape.

A young woman plopped down on the pew in front with her four squiggling children. The three little boys, all of whom appeared as if they would attempt an escape any minute, dressed and looked identical. Each sported a shirt, trousers, and a little red clip-on tie. The ties each dangled in different directions, and the little tabs designed to fit under the collar splayed out on the sides. The boy's shoes wore a fresh layer of mud, and they kept scraping the dirt off the soles and sides by rubbing their feet on the pew in front.

The fourth child, an infant girl, protested vehemently about her frilly pink dress. Her shrieking reminded me of an old civil defense siren. It started as a low moan, then came in great waves of overwhelming sound, only to subside and begin anew. The ear-shattering symphony of discontent continued until the harried mother finally forced her three little Attilas to sit and shoved a pacifier into the baby's mouth.

No sooner had the cacaphony before me subsided than I heard another disturbance, a strange sort of groaning. It sounded a little like a car that won't quite start.

Turning my head, I saw a man seated in a wheelchair. He slumped to his right with a blanket over his knees. His faded sports shirt lay open at the throat. His scant hair flew this way and that, and his skin bore a greyish-blue tinge. His left arm rested uselessly in his lap, contorted into little more than a claw. With a vacant gleam, he stared at everything and nothing at the same time. Once he looked over at me and I smiled a little. What else could I do? I was embarrassed he caught me looking at him, but he gave no acknowledgment. All the while his head bobbed up and down, and he continued making that odd, moaning noise.

The choir's entrance ended my surveillance of the congregation. I could not help but compare their meandering to the impressive and moving procession of my church's choir. Each Christmas Eve, for as long as I can remember, soprano, alto, tenor, and bass have marched down the center aisle singing "Adeste Fidelis" supported by pipe organ, handbells, and brass.

That this choir lacked robes hardly surprised me. From what I'd seen, vestments would have seemed out of place. But I found their lack of organization appalling. They just wandered in. They exhibited no uniform dress—two even wore overalls. One choir member waved to someone in the congregation.

The service began, but I could not get into it. Where was the dignity, the majesty, the pageantry? No one had a bulletin, and no one appeared to know what would happen next. I'm sure the minister wasn't making things up as he went along, but it surely seemed like it. Long, awkward pauses continually ruptured what little flow anyone could generate, and at one point the minister actually had to signal the pianist to play.

When we stood to sing, I couldn't find a hymnal. *No problem,* I thought, *I know all the carols by heart.* I guess I expected "Silent Night" or "Hark, the Herald Angels Sing," but the pianist launched into some bouncy tune about Jesus' garments and myrrh and teardrops. I'd never heard this before, but by the time we hit the third stanza, I could stumble through the chorus:

> Out of the ivory palaces,
> Into a world of woe—
> Only His great, eternal love
> Made my Savior go.[7]

We merged into another equally obscure tune that began "In a cave, a lonely stable, Christ our Lord was born."

I like to sing. My voice isn't anything to write home about, but I can carry a tune, and I love Christmas music. But what was this?

Once again I thought about my church, the pipe organ

leading, the overflowing congregation singing "Joy to the World" and "O Come, All Ye Faithful." What a tumultuous sound! Ah, God's people making a joyous and harmonious sound. *That* is worship.

We sat down after the third one, "Wonderful, wonderful Jesus! He is my friend, true to the end." I guess they just wanted to get all the singing over at once.

The choir started digging around for their music, but before they sang a note, I knew they would sound abysmal. I was right.

Two women of enormous girth dominated the sound. They exploded with imprecise vocal instruments and vibratos into which one could maneuver a good-sized truck. A lone tenor screeched out among the clamor. The poor fellow possessed the heart of an eagle but feet of clay. He longed to soar to the stratosphere of the scale, but he always managed to fall a half-step short of the intended pitch. The other men sang very quietly, almost as if fearful of being heard. Some mumbled the melody several octaves below the original. The others improvised various parts that coincided neither with the piano nor with one another.

Oddly enough, they sang "The Old Rugged Cross." What happened to "Lo, How a Rose E'er Blooming"? I longed for "Jesu, Joy of Man's Desiring." Each Christmas Eve, our home choir performs moving classical selections accompanied by a string quartet or a harpsichord. Here it was, Christmas Eve, and I was "on a hill far away."

When the choir sat, I started to leave, but the minister rose to deliver the sermon. He was a slightly built man in his sixties, with a craggy face and small, gold-rimmed spectacles that threatened at any minute to slip off his hawklike nose. He spoke in a soft and quavery voice. When he said, "Let us pray," it sounded more like a plea for mercy than a summons to approach almighty God.

The cuffs of his shiny, worn suit trousers stood well above a pair of scuffed and battered brown shoes. And he prayed, "Lord, these are your words. I hope I say them right. Amen."

The sermon could not have lasted as long as it seemed, but

by this time my cynicism had climbed to everestine heights and my patience all but disappeared. I thought it would never end.

Throughout the course of the service, the big guy next to me continued his attempt to free his neck from the discomfort of his cast-iron collar. During the sermon he redoubled his efforts. His gyrations, combined with the stifling heat (they turned off the fans when the choir warbled), the wiggling kids, the frantic mother, and the spasmodically screaming infant all made me very nervous.

The sermon, what little of it I caught, struck me as woefully weak: brave Joseph, faithful Mary, little Baby, meek and mild, adoring shepherds, come to Jesus.

The wheelchair-bound invalid kept on groaning. Apparently no one else noticed or minded, but his noise grew louder and louder. I began to fidget. I could not get comfortable. The pew lacked cushioning and my dress started sticking to my back. Sweat fell into my eyes, my head pounded, and I started to feel queasy.

As soon as the service ended, I bolted for the door. I snuck out a side entrance to avoid the preacher. Thanking my lucky stars to be out in the fresh air again without anyone asking my opinion of the service, I made my way toward the parking lot.

I had one foot off the curb when I turned to read the sign at the front of the church:

Meadowbrook Presbyterian Church
Established 1948
Edmund L. Wilcox, Pastor

A verse of Scripture ran below the preacher's name. As I read it, my heart rose in my throat. Suddenly I felt very ashamed—not of my fine clothes, or of the church in which I routinely worship, or of the magnificent organ or of the professional choir. I grew ashamed of myself and of my conviction that those things are essential to the meaningful worship of God. I'd so concerned myself with worship's peripherals that I'd ignored worship's purpose.

The folk of Meadowbrook seemed simple, but they were undeniably sincere. They hardly showed up in the fanciest of clothes, but they managed to approach the throne of God in the finest of spirits. Their church never would be confused with a cathedral, but then, we were worshipping a child originally adored in a stable.

Oh, yes, numerous distractions abounded. The invalid communicated only with his groaning, but whomever brought him knew where he wanted to be on Christmas Eve. The children annoyed me, but what better place for a mother to bring her brood. For my part the service lacked a little—it lacked a lot—but everything transpired in a spirit of praise and devotion.

It slowly dawned on me that although I had long championed the equality of all men and women, it wasn't until that precise moment I realized all worship is equal. Some services are more formal, to be sure. Others may make a bigger impression. Certain types of services mean more to certain types of people.

But from the Latin invocations of Saint Peter's to the sing-song style of a traditional black preacher, from the formality of a mainstream Protestant service to the relaxed atmosphere of a vesper gathering outdoors, from the enthusiasm of a large tent meeting to the quiet thoughtfulness of family devotions, all Christians do the same thing in worship.

Tonight people all over the world sang different songs to different tunes. They said different prayers and exercised different customs. They wore different outfits and followed different rites. But tonight of all nights, every single Christian in all creation heard the same announcement:

For to you is born this day in the city
of David a Savior, who is Christ the Lord.[8]

I read the sign again:

Meadowbrook Presbyterian Church
Established 1948
Edmund L. Wilcox, Pastor

"Wherever two or three are gathered in my name, there I am in the midst of them."

I headed toward the car. A hand touched my shoulder, and I turned to find Pastor Wilcox.

"Madame," he said softly, "I noticed you in the congregation. We don't get too many visitors. I just wanted to tell you how glad we were you came to be with us on this very special evening. I hope you were blessed by our worship."

I shook his hand and looked into his tired and kindly face. "I was, sir." I answered. "I really was. Merry Christmas."

The Man We Do Not Know

Call me what you will. What makes you any different? You didn't think I knew, did you? But I've heard what you said: "penny-pincher," "mercenary," "hard-hearted." I've read the stories about how I was too busy, too impressed with my other guests to take in a struggling couple.

You speak rudely of me, but you've never even heard my name. I'm just "the innkeeper"—a title instead of a person.

Well, I *do* have a name: Nathan. This still doesn't tell you much because you've never seen my face, have you? You all keep reproductions of my stable and my manger in your homes, but no one cherishes an image of Nathan the innkeeper.

I have a story as well—one you've probably never heard.

* * * * *

A lot of people hated the census. They thought it was a real pain, too much bother; but our clan welcomed it gladly. We all hadn't been together in five long years. I'll admit I have no use for the Romans, but I felt strangely indebted to the emperor for scheduling an enrollment requiring us to organize a family reunion.

My brothers, sisters, cousins, and children—thirty-five in all—came from all over.

I, the eldest, played the role of patriarch to the hilt: exaggerating my age to the very young, dispensing sage advice to the newlyweds (and anyone else within earshot), and issuing as many orders as I could invent.

We all crammed into my house, which was attached to the side of the inn my father left me. It was a large house—the Lord has blessed me—but so many people could make any place shrink. We loved it anyway.

The inn overflowed, too. While the other lodge caters to the rich and flashy, my establishment, the smaller of two public houses in Bethlehem, attracts the more sedate. I run a quiet, clean place with a family atmosphere.

I'd never seen it so full. My three employees scurried back and forth all night, struggling to please everyone, but most of the lodgers remained courteous and patient.

When my brother, Caleb, and his family arrived from Joppa, the celebration began in earnest. My wife and daughters had cooked all day, and the moment Caleb's crew crossed the threshold we assaulted the table.

What a dinner! We ate, talked, and laughed ourselves silly.

We raised such a racket, the traveler had to come into the house and lead me away from the festivities so I could hear him. He called himself Joseph, from Nazareth—seventy miles due north—a long haul.

He towered over me, with massive arms and a barrel chest. Flecks of grey salted his beard, and while he talked, he opened and closed his hands as if he would have been more comfortable with something in his grasp.

I don't know why he bothered stopping. The "no vacancy" sign hung very clearly from my front gate. Besides, they had room at the other inn—Bethlehem's no metropolis—and Joseph must have passed it on his way into town. But either the rates or the clientele made him shy away.

Despite what you've heard, I wanted to help. Joseph and his young bride looked pitiful. Pain creased her face so regularly, even I could tell she would give birth soon. How she made the trip on the poor, stringy-legged excuse for a donkey upon which she fidgeted I have yet to figure out.

Money had nothing to do with my refusal. I have never turned away a traveler because of insufficient funds. I simply had nowhere to put them—not even on the floor. But I could not let them go unattended, either. So after sending for Rebecca, the midwife, I led them to the stable.

Early in the evening the word of the birth arrived. A boy—blessed be the name of the Lord—a son, an heir. Both he and his mother were doing fine. Normally we might have rushed to see the proud parents to celebrate and congratulate them. But Rebecca said the mother seemed tired and suggested we wait until morning.

* * * * *

No one would ever mistake Isaac for a genius, but he carried a well-earned reputation as a very trustworthy shepherd. So when I discovered him at my door, I had cause for concern. Only some calamity could separate him from his fluffy charges.

Then I noticed the others: Simeon, Ezra, Zorbed, Joshua, and one or two more.

"Where is the Child?"

News travels quickly—especially news indicating the opportunity for a celebration. They'd play some prank first, sort of a country custom, by imitating jackals outside the door in an attempt to frighten. Then they'd bounce in with songs and dancing and a gift or two. No harm intended. If Joseph wished them to leave, they would depart without a quarrel.

But no one looked particularly festive. They all stood quietly at my door as if awaiting instructions. Joshua even seemed sober for the first time I could remember. I mean he didn't weave or slur his speech, but he still told a pretty wild tale.

Joshua went on and on about something he called "the vision." The others tried to shut him up, but Joshua would not be denied. Finally, the little group shuffled toward the stable, leaving Joshua behind to weave his latest.

It seems little Sarah had come up from the village with the report of the birth. Joshua claimed that just as she told them the news the sky caught on fire, and the winds ripped across the hills. Sounded like music, he said.

How long it all lasted Joshua couldn't exactly remember, but as soon as everything calmed down, all the shepherds decided to head for Bethlehem to find the newborn baby.

Then Joshua began his tale all over again.

When I'd had all I could stomach in one session, I sent him on his way to the stable with a warning about what his wine consumption was doing to his mind and then went inside.

The evening whipped by. When I wasn't rehashing old stories with my relatives or playing games with the children, I had to take more food to this lodger or another blanket to that one.

What a grand night! I never got tired—there was too much to do. I had a loving family and a booming business—who could ask for more?

Yet in the back of my mind, the memory of a child born in a stable gnawed at me. Was he warm? Was he all right? Would he make it through the night?

The uproar in the house continued as I slipped out the back door and across the moonlit courtyard.

Isaac and his friends obviously decided to spend the evening, and the stable bulged with people. Silence encased the little room and I crept toward the little family as unobtrusively as I could.

I didn't see anything wrong with the child's crib. Babies had slept in mangers before and would again—what more obvious place in a barn? Maybe the bed seemed a little crude, but the clean, dry straw kept the boy as safe and comfortable as possible.

Halfway to the manger I realized everyone was staring at the child. No one moved, but every eye in the place riveted on the small boy resting in the stone trough at his mother's elbow.

No one blocked my way to the makeshift crib. I meant no harm—my only weapon the lamb's wool comforter I carried under my arm.

I draped the blanket over the sleeping child as gently as

I could, and buried both ends in the straw on either side of him so the night air would not seep in. And there, looking into the face of a little one sleeping the sleep known only to children, I could hear the echo of the rabbi's voice from sabbath past:

> "For to us a child is born,
>   to us a son is given;
> And the government will be upon
>   his shoulder,
> and his name will be called
> 'Wonderful Counselor, Mighty God,
> Everlasting Father, Prince of Peace.'
> Of the increase of his government
> and of peace
> there will be no end. . . .[9]

They never missed me in the house. Oh, the celebration went on, but everyone had more than enough stories to go around, and the children soon fell tired of their games and shuffled off to bed. My wife attended to the guests with her typical efficiency, and none of them could complain of neglect.

But I, Nathan the innkeeper, passed the night on my knees in the stable, thanking God for the life of a most unusual baby boy.

My family reunion demanded my attention, but I took time to see Him. My wife and I were entertaining, but I made the effort to worship Him. I had a lot of pressing business, but abandoned it to tend to the Child.

I could not find any room in my inn, but I made room for them in my heart. And I pray you will, too.

Notes

[1]The poem, "A Song in the Heart," was written by Irene Vance Olsen, Mr. Fogartie's great aunt.
[2]1 Corinthians 11:27–28, RSV
[3]"Once in Royal David's City," lyrics by Cecil Frances Alexander.
[4]Luke 2:7, RSV
[5]Luke 2:10–11, KJV
[6]Luke 2:8–11, KJV
[7]"Ivory Palaces" by Henry Barraclough, copyright 1915. Renewal 1943 by Hope Publishing Company, Carol Stream, Illinois 60188. Used by permission.
[8]Luke 2:11, RSV
[9]Isaiah 9:6–7, RSV

DATE DUE

Anderson

~15697759

ILL
11/28/94

NOV. 2 2 1994

NOV 2 5 1997

12-11-97